If you were an
Adjective

by Michael Dahl

illustrated by Sara Gray

PICTURE WINDOW BOOKS
Minneapolis, Minnesota

adjective (adj) a word that describes or modifies a noun or pronoun

Looking for adjectives? Watch for the big, colorful words in the example sentences.

Editor: Christianne Jones
Designer: Nathan Gassman
Page Production: Tracy Kaehler
Creative Director: Keith Griffin
Editorial Director: Carol Jones
The illustrations in this book were created with acrylics.

Picture Window Books
151 Good Counsel Drive
P.O. Box 669
Mankato, MN 56002-0669
877-845-8392
www.picturewindowbooks.com

Printed in China.

Library of Congress Cataloging-in-Publication Data
Dahl, Michael.
If you were an adjective / by Michael Dahl ; illustrated by Sara Gray.
p. cm. — (Word fun)
Includes bibliographical references and index.
ISBN 978-1-4048-1356-4 (hardcover)
ISBN 978-1-4048-1982-5 (paperback)
1. English language—Adjective—Juvenile literature.
I. Gray, Sara, ill. II. Title. III. Series.
PE1241.D34 2006
428.1—dc22
                                    2005021856

Special thanks to our advisers for their expertise:

Rosemary G. Palmer, Ph.D., Department of Literacy
College of Education, Boise State University

Susan Kesselring, M.A., Literacy Educator
Rosemount—Apple Valley—Eagan (Minnesota) School District

If you were an adjective ...

... you
would be

COLORFUL!

BRILLIANT!

DAZZLING!

FEATHERY!

MANY-LEGGED!

SLIMY!

If you were an adjective, you would work side by side with nouns. A noun names a person, place, or thing. As an adjective, you would be busy describing nouns.

An elephant is a noun.

If you were an adjective, you would tell us about the elephant.

The **GRAY** elephant is **GIGANTIC** and **WET**. The **SPARKLING** water cools down the **HOT** elephant.

If you were an adjective, you would tell us how a person, place, or thing looks.

The SLENDER swimmer snaps a photo of

the **ENORMOUS** whale in the **DEEP,** **BLUE** water.

9

If you were an adjective, you would describe things.

The **TINY** kittens are **FLUFFY.**

The **LITTLE** piglets are **PUDGY** and **PINK.**

The **COLORFUL** peacock's tail is **BIG** and **BRIGHT.**

If you were an adjective, you would describe how something sounds.

The howler monkey is **LOUD!**

The boa's movement is SILENT.

The **QUIET** mouse watches and waits.

If you were an adjective, you would describe how something feels.

The alligator's back is RIDGED and BUMPY.

If you were an adjective, you would describe how something behaves.

The **FEARLESS** plover is **CAREFUL** when it picks at the alligator's teeth.

If you were an adjective, you might be a proper adjective.

A proper adjective describes a specific object and is always capitalized.

In winter, the **Arctic** fox's coat turns white to blend in with the snow of the **Alaskan** tundra.

19

If you were an adjective, you could compare things. You would change your ending to show how things are different.

You would be a comparative adjective if you compared two things.

The turtle is **SMALL.**

The tree frog is **SMALLER.**

You would be a superlative adjective if you compared three things.

The lion is **FAST.**

You could be **BAD,**

WORSE, WORST, or

GOOD,

BETTER, BEST...

... if you were an adjective.

Fun with Adjectives

Directions: Write your name from top to bottom on a piece of paper. Now, think of adjectives that describe you. Use the letters in your name as the first letters of the adjectives. For example, you might write:

Mysterious
Intelligent
Creative
Happy
Athletic
Easy-going
Loud

Then, see if you can find adjectives to describe your friends.

Fact: If you look up an adjective in the dictionary, you will see the abbreviation "adj" next to it. The "adj" stands for adjective.

Glossary

gigantic—huge

noun—a person, place, or thing

plover—a type of shorebird with a short, hard bill

pudgy—short and fat

ridged—bumpy

swift—a type of bird related to hummingbirds

tundra—an area of flat or rolling plains with no trees

To Learn More

More Books to Read

Cleary, Brian P. *Hairy, Scary, Ordinary: What Is an Adjective?* Minneapolis: Carolrhoda Books, 2000.

Doudna, Kelly. *Adjectives.* Edina, Minn.: Abdo Pub., 2001.

Heinrichs, Ann. *Adjectives.* Chanhassen, Minn.: Child's World, 2004.

On the Web

FactHound offers a safe, fun way to find Web sites related to topics in this book. All of the sites on FactHound have been researched by our staff.

1. Visit www.facthound.com
2. Type in this special code: 140481356X
3. Click on the FETCH IT button.

Your trusty FactHound will fetch the best sites for you!

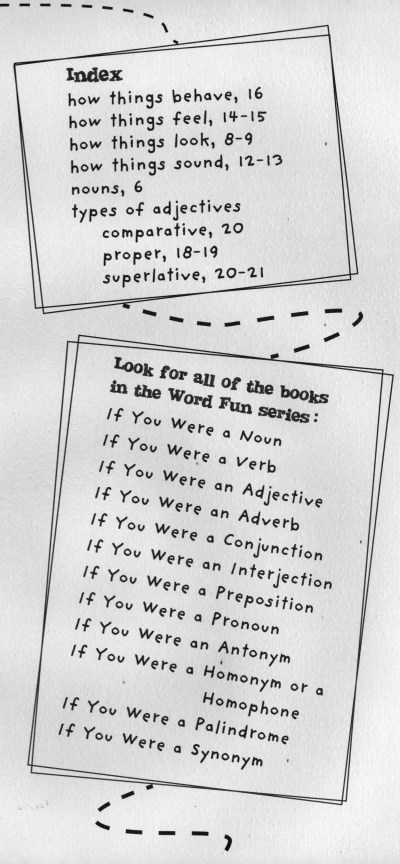

Look for all of the books in the Word Fun series:

If You Were a Noun
If You Were a Verb
If You Were an Adjective
If You Were an Adverb
If You Were a Conjunction
If You Were an Interjection
If You Were a Preposition
If You Were a Pronoun
If You Were an Antonym
If You Were a Homonym or a Homophone
If You Were a Palindrome
If You Were a Synonym